# Mysticism for All

Especially for Parents

# Mysticism for All

## Especially for Parents

Karel Weinfurter

Translated by Kytka Hilmarová

Mysticism for All, Especially for Parents. Copyright © 2023 by Kytka Hilmarová

All rights reserved. No part of this publication may be reproduced, distributed, or transmitted in any form or by any means, including photocopying, recording, or other electronic or mechanical methods, without the prior written permission of the publisher, except in the case of brief quotations embodied in critical reviews and specific other noncommercial uses permitted by copyright law. For permission requests or information about special discounts or bulk purchases, please contact:

Czech Revival Publishing.
www.czechrevival.com
US+ 727-238-7884

The views expressed in this work are the author's own and may not reflect the opinions or policies of any organization or individual. The author's personal experiences and opinions are shared for entertainment and educational purposes. Readers are encouraged to form their own conclusions based on the content presented. The author assumes no responsibility for the reader's actions. References to people, organizations, or events are based on the author's translation, recollection, and/or interpretation. This work does not provide professional advice, and readers should consult experts in relevant fields for guidance.

Library of Congress Cataloging-in-Publication Data

Weinfurter, Karel 1867-1942
Hilmarova, Kytka 1964-
         Mysticism for All Especially for Parents. / Kytka Hilmarová

Summary: "Mysticism for All (Especially for Parents)" is a captivating translation of Karel Weinfurter's Czech book "Mystika všem: (zvláště rodičům)." This edition allows readers to delve into Weinfurter's profound teachings. Exploring the realms of mysticism, Weinfurter provides valuable insights and guidance, particularly on parents. This translation brings Weinfurter's teachings to life, offering readers a deeper understanding of mysticism's relevance to their lives.

ISBN-13: 978-1-943103-28-7

1. BODY, MIND & SPIRIT / Mysticism 2. RELIGION / Mysticism 3. SELF-HELP / Spiritual

*Open your heart and embark on a profound journey of self-discovery, for within the realms of mysticism lies the hidden wisdom that can illuminate your path and awaken your soul.*

# Table of Contents

Preface ................................................................. 1

Introduction ......................................................... 7

Chapter I ............................................................ 21

Chapter II .......................................................... 29

Chapter III ......................................................... 41

Chapter IV ......................................................... 59

Chapter V .......................................................... 67

About the Author ............................................. 107

Translator's Note ............................................. 117

About the Translator ....................................... 119

# Preface

I am pleased to present my translation of the book, Mystika všem (zvláště rodičům), which immediately caught my attention with its focus on parents. Upon discovering Karel Weinfurter's extensive body of work, I was captivated by his unwavering commitment to exploring and sharing spiritual wisdom. Hailing from Prague, Weinfurter dedicated his life to delving into the enigmatic realms of mysticism and the occult.

Within the pages of this book, you will have the opportunity to delve into the profound insights of Karel Weinfurter as he explores the interpretation of miracles, mystical experiences, and the hidden dimensions of reality. Weinfurter's relentless pursuit of understanding the spiritual nature of human existence is evident throughout his writings. With an impressive collection of eight dozen titles bearing his name, Weinfurter's contributions are extensive. It is worth noting that while some of these titles are pamphlets containing extracts from his more comprehensive works, they still offer valuable insights.

A significant turning point in Weinfurter's life occurred when his book "The Fiery Bush, or the Revealed Mystical Path" was published on Easter in 1923. Little did he anticipate the profound impact it would have, quickly capturing the attention and interest of readers and selling out in no time. It is not only Weinfurter's original works that leave a lasting impression; his translations are equally noteworthy. Having translated over three hundred books, he introduced esteemed figures in mysticism to the Czech audience. Notable among his translations are the first Czech renditions of the works of Indian saint Raman Maharshi, Meister Eckhart's two-volume sermons and parables, de Molinos's "Spiritual Leader," and selected writings by Swami Vivekananda and Madame (Helena) Blavatsky.

In addition to his translations and scholarly work, Weinfurter's literary contributions encompassed a diverse range of genres. He authored eight collections of fairy tales and short stories, which gained recognition through publication in contemporary periodicals. Furthermore, his memoirs, widely referenced in the field, offer valuable insights into the early stages of alternative spiritual research in our country and provide intriguing glimpses into the lives of notable figures such as Julius Zeyer, Jaroslav Vrchlický, and Gustav Meyrink, among others.

Weinfurter's teachings were deeply influenced by a wide range of mystical traditions. He drew inspiration from Western mystics, including Meister Eckhart and his followers Heinrich Suso, Johannes Tauler, Jan van Ruysbroek, Thomas à Kempis, and Madame Guyon. He also explored the writings of heretical thinkers like Jakob Böhme, as well as the quietists Miguel de Molinos, John Pordage, and Jane Leade. In his quest for knowledge, Weinfurter delved into the works of mystics such as Karl von Eckhartshausen and the freemason Johann Baptist Kerning. Furthermore, he immersed himself in the wisdom of Indian mystics and yogis, studying the teachings of Ramakrishna and corresponding with his disciples. He also engaged with the contemporary mystic Raman Maharshi, recognizing their contributions to the rich tradition of Indian Vedanta.

Weinfurter viewed mysticism and yoga as interchangeable paths, both centered on the silent contemplation of humanity's spiritual and divine essence. He held the belief that Indian science, particularly yoga, possessed a higher level of philosophical sophistication, untainted by Western materialism and the societal transformations of civilization. Weinfurter fully embraced the principles of karma and reincarnation, going so far as to recognize Jesus as one of the Avatars, divine incarnations that have manifested throughout different epochs in history.

Weinfurter emphasized that, in his view, mysticism transcends mere opinions and rests on objective facts. The path of mystical maturation reveals unmistakable signs, whether one follows the Western or Eastern traditions. Mysticism, in and of itself, is not the ultimate aim but rather a vehicle for attaining profound knowledge. This knowledge may manifest as contemplation, union with the divine, realization, nirvana, or the absolute—various terms used to describe the pinnacle of spiritual experience. Weinfurter underscored that the ultimate significance lies in achieving the goal itself, rather than fixating solely on the journey toward it.

This translated book serves as a relatively short and accessible read, providing an introduction to mysticism. It offers a glimpse into the profound insights of Karel Weinfurter and explores the realms of spirituality and the mysteries of existence.

I sincerely hope that within these pages, you will find joy and enlightenment. May Weinfurter's profound wisdom and exploration of mystical paths resonate with your spiritual journey. As you delve into his writings, may you uncover hidden truths, expand your consciousness, and embrace the divinity within.

# Introduction

This book is dedicated to parents who have experienced mysticism as the culmination of all religions, who practice mystical exercises and engage in practical mysticism. It is dedicated to them with the aim of guiding their children more easily on the mystical path, starting from early childhood and from the age of seven to practical mysticism, namely mystical exercises.

Before embarking on this work, the writer was repeatedly asked and urged by parents to write guidelines that parents could follow in raising their children. It is a challenging task, but on the other hand, immensely delightful because its purpose is to fulfill the words of our highest Guide and Lord Jesus Christ:

*"Let the little children come to me, for theirs is the kingdom of heaven."*

These words of the Lord Jesus Christ were also a guiding principle for me to undertake this work after some hesitation, which is intended to guide our little brothers and sisters on the true Path, those who are only entering the whirlpool and struggle of life after years. They need timely rescue when they have not yet experienced this world's errors, falsehoods, and temptations so that their innocent souls may be led to the truth. Thus, they are given an impenetrable armor to fight against the forces that dominate this dark world, this immense maze, from which it is so difficult to find an exit without a guiding thread!

And what else can serve as such a golden thread and armor, if not the imparting of correct beliefs about God, about man, his origin and mission, and about science, which today corrupts everything and is essentially a temptation and a Babylonian tower, boasting of its external structure, but lacking actual value?

It is mysticism, this veiled truth in every religion, a truth always forgotten and lost in time, but a truth that, like an eternal spring, can never be permanently extinguished but always emerges and appears unexpectedly in another place to refresh and strengthen the thirsty and prepare them for the further struggle for the ultimate freedom and liberation that can be achieved on earth - the freedom of the spirit and the conquest of victory over the whole world.

Do not be afraid to instill mystical truths in your already young children, for know that God desires it and will bless you for it, as it is through this that you fulfill your foremost duty toward your beloved ones.

Nothing else matters to them more than the best education in other areas, your greatest care and diligence, if you were to deny them knowledge of the eternal law and fail to tell them how they should conceive of God, their Creator, and where they should seek Him and how to find Him.

Please think of the hardships you save your dear children, the errors you protect them from, and how you ease their discovery of the one true Path when you gradually tell them, from a tender age, what you yourself know, what you have become convinced of, and what is most sacred to you.

Remember how long you yourselves wandered, how much you had to experience and endure before, by the grace of the Spirit, you found the Path and satisfaction and the true purpose of human life. Master Rama Krishna expressed more than once that the true purpose of every human being's life is the search for and finding of God, thus the rebirth in the Spirit. We are not here for anything else. But we must know how to seek God and where to seek Him.

Remember how you fell from one error to another, how you perhaps sank into materialistic teachings denying everything spiritual, and how happy you were when mysticism opened your eyes! Remember again how you were captivated by the enticing snares of spiritualism or theosophy or other incorrect teachings of the occult, which may unveil the veil to some extent but lead you behind it, instead of to the spiritual Sun, to new and new mazes and corridors from which it is not easy to escape!

And remember that day when the light dawned upon you and how you rejoiced in having discovered the ultimate truth, beyond which there is no other, which is as pure as crystal and has the power to awaken love and faith in God in every soul, and which also showed you the path that leads directly to the inner sanctuary!

And also remember how many of you had to undergo fierce battles with your old beliefs, how your inner being resisted accepting the mystical teaching, how you suffered mentally and physically before the fight was won before you gained the conviction that mysticism is actually what you were seeking and not finding, and what finally redeemed you from all doubts and the spiritual struggles of transformation.

And when you remember this, you must undoubtedly say to yourselves that you will strive with all your might to protect your little ones, your dearest ones, from the impending sinking into the same errors and false beliefs that once engulfed you, which held your souls in heavy chains.

The soul of a child is like an unwritten, pure sheet of paper. It can be impressed with anything we desire. The soul of a child is an empty and pure chalice into which we can pour both crystal-clear water and a poisonous drink. The chalice, in its trustfulness, accepts both equally.

Do you want, perhaps, the chalice of your child's soul to be filled with worldly teachings, for that soul to be poisoned with disbelief and scientific idolatry, and for it to have to struggle for a long, long time to rid itself of that potent poison? Or do you believe the church's religious teachings are sufficient to protect your child from errors?

Just look around today's society and delve deeper into the souls of today's children. You will be astonished at how weak religious education is and how it cannot provide children - and no one else - with truly solid support. Or have you forgotten how you also had a religious school education once and how you still struggled in the darkness, how you were lukewarm in spiritual matters - because you lacked deeper instruction and, above all, tangible evidence of God and His powers, which were given to you only through mystical practice?

However, you must not take away from your children their trust in teachers and education in general. Still, you must deepen and supplement it according to your own convictions! Child-rearing today is just as flawed as before, if not worse, because certain political factions are even trying to introduce politics into schools, which is the greatest poison for children and adults. Therefore, politics or so-called class hatred are the greatest poison for a child's soul, and anyone who seeks to destroy children in this way is the greatest criminal. You must confront this poison especially and vigorously, always addressing it immediately on a case-by-case basis so that the poison is not absorbed.

However, these are complex matters that cannot be detailed in writing. Your own conscience will guide you safely if you follow your spiritual intuition and the general guidelines provided in this book.

As for the age at which a child can engage in practical exercises, according to the student Kernigov Kolba, who left us the valuable book "Rebirth," it can begin as soon as the child reaches the age of seven. At this age, the child can easily understand the exercises. Since the seventh year of life is when the soul begins to unfold, it is also the springtime of human life, the best time to introduce practical mystical teachings to the young soul.

No instruction given to a child at this time will be lost throughout their entire life, no guidance will be forgotten, and everything that you sow into the child's soul after age seven must bear its fruit.

But even before that, you must gently reference God and His presence within the human heart in your conversations with the child. This truth is the most important for everyone, including children. It can be relied upon at all times and under all circumstances.

Most children are curious and inquisitive, often asking their parents or adults various questions. These questions are often profound and challenging, leaving parents at a loss because they do not know the correct answers.

Children mistakenly believe that parents and adults must know everything and ask them because every child is curious and eager to learn. And once a child realizes that there is something called human science, their curiosity knows no bounds. They believe that educated people must have all the answers and know everything. The child does not know that science itself knows nothing at all. After all, it does not understand the foundations of creation, and, most importantly, it seeks to solve everything with external reason, which is finite and limited, and without God, whose knowledge is infinite and unlimited.

And here lies an immense reservoir of nourishment and knowledge for the child's soul - namely, in mysticism and occult teachings.

Let's give a small example. Children are taught so-called "civil morality," which teaches that it is necessary for a person to always be honest, sincere, reasonable, and fulfill their duties toward others, the state, the country, and so on.

But when a child asks its overwhelming "Why?" questions, civil morality has no other answers than that a person must be so because, without these good qualities, they would not succeed themselves, their family, their nation, the state, or all of humanity. There is no other explanation.

But when we can tell the child, for example: "A person must be so because a person is the temple of God, because they have a spark of the eternal Creator within them, and this spark must develop into a flame so that the person, permeated by God, can know and accomplish everything. And this can only happen in a vessel that is pure and free from evil qualities!" then we give the child a satisfying answer, and also the only true one.

We should not hesitate to tell the child, in response to certain questions about creation, that science does not know the answer, that humanity is still groping in the dark, and that only the enlightenment given by God will solve such mysteries of nature or humanity. The child will then view science with greater sobriety and not consider scholars as true adepts who must know everything, as is, unfortunately, the case in much of the world today!

Similarly, we can use occult teachings to help both the child and ourselves in addressing all other matters because evasive answers, which parents are often forced to give to children, leave a certain emptiness and dissatisfaction in the parents' souls, resulting from the imposed dishonesty.

And at this point, I would like to draw parents' attention to the fact that a child is essentially a little occultist. Their thirst for occult knowledge is evident in their fondness for fairy tales and everything related to the occult world. Fairy tales, in particular, will be a valuable aid in teaching children about occult laws, as will be explained later. The invisible world is much closer to children than adults because the child's soul has recently returned from the invisible realm to assume a body as its instrument. There are vague memories of the spiritual, disembodied life, and that is why children eagerly listen to stories about fairies, wizards, magic, and similar things. Educators may explain this with the immense imagination of children, but this explanation is insufficient. Why wouldn't they focus on other things if it were just imagination? Why only subjects related to occult knowledge?

Those who want to lead a child toward mysticism must possess sufficient knowledge of this subject themselves. That is a prerequisite. A teacher must have a good understanding of what they want to teach. Children receive nothing similar in school, so this task falls solely on the parents. They must be familiar with fundamental mystical texts and have the subject matter ingrained in their blood.

Among such books, I include the following: Bhagavad Gita, Rama Krishna (both volumes), Kernig's "The Path to Immortality," and "The Fiery Bush" (Part I). However, it is clear that we can also read passages from the New Testament to children, especially certain statements of Jesus Christ and His miracles (splendid examples of mystical powers), as well as select verses from the letters of St. Paul. Of course, everything must be carefully chosen. In complex cases, I recommend that parents obtain my extensive work: "The Bible in the Light of Mysticism," where they will find explanations of all the secret sayings of the New Testament that theologians and other scholars deliberately overlook because they simply cannot explain them. Of course, a mystical key is required to interpret such statements—a mere external reason is utterly inadequate in these cases. But such a key is only given to a disciple of mysticism who has sufficiently evolved spiritually.

Regarding all occult questions, I consider the most valuable and comprehensible source to be the book "Secret Forces of Nature and Man," which I published a few years ago.

# Chapter I

**First Mystical Teachings**

Thoughtful and discerning parents gradually instill mystical teachings in their children from the age of four, as soon as they begin to explore their surroundings and their intellect begins to develop.

However, this does not mean that parents should instruct their beloved child on profound mystical matters but rather instill the fundamental principles of mysticism from the beginning. For example, children are told that God is in heaven, and they point to the sky. This is a fundamental and significant mistake. From the beginning, the child must be taught the correct understanding that God is everywhere and in everything, in every creature from the greatest to the smallest, in every flower and tree, in every thing, be it large or small, living or non-living.

God is an invisible Spirit, the highest power that manifests itself in diverse ways throughout nature, both on earth and in the universe, primarily in human beings. God resides hidden and invisible in the human heart, yet all-powerful and supremely good.

The greatest mistake is made by priests of all Christian churches when they constantly repeat to believers, whether adults or children, that God is in heaven. This misleads people, causing them to seek God outside themselves, somewhere in the universe. While it is true that the correct prayer can reach God in this way, it is never as secure and certain as when our thoughts are directed to the spiritual heart. It is necessary to guide even the youngest child in directing their prayer to the center of their chest. This will save them much effort in later concentration exercises because the child's thoughts will already form a particular path into the inner being at an early age, which adults must forge and dig with great effort.

Many mothers and fathers tell their children, for example, during a thunderstorm and thunder, "God is angry!" They say the same thing to a child when they have made a mistake. This is incorrect. The child then imagines God as a person or being similar to humans, with all their flaws and various moods, such as anger. God can never be angry with anyone, nor can He be offended by anyone, as some priests claim when speaking of sin. No sin can offend God because He is elevated above all human actions and remains unmoved—only the highest love and the longing for Him can move God to bestow His grace upon humanity.

I touched upon a particularly favored word in Christianity that should be entirely rejected and replaced with another word. That word is "sin." What is sin? It is a violation of God's law, a falling from ignorance. Churches instruct their priests to constantly speak to people about sins, not about the grace of the Lord, which we should constantly seek. According to the Church's teachings and dogmas, humanity is immersed in a sea of sins and nothing but sins. When Master Rama Krishna once read a particular Christian book, he was astonished by this and said that the constant repetition of the word "sin" truly stains the soul and that people should instead be led to pray: "Lord, I have made a mistake, please forgive me, and I promise never to commit it again!"

The Indians have a completely different term instead of the word "sin," which fundamentally explains why people sin. It is the word "avidya," which means ignorance. Christ also used this word, particularly in a significant instance when he said, "Father, forgive them, for they know not what they do!"

At a later age, around the age of six, we can tell children more about God, and especially at this point, it is necessary to cultivate the idea of God as the highest and most perfect being, as a radiant Spirit, as the Lord of all, filled with the highest love. The child may have this concept externally, but we also teach them that the same God who invisibly rules the entire universe is also present in every human being.
The best concept of God for a Christian child is either the likeness of Jesus Christ or the Virgin Mary. Especially the idea of the Virgin Mary is recommended for children, as it allows the young mystic to perceive the Virgin Mary as their great, eternal, and all-powerful Mother, making it easier for them to understand the love that one must feel toward

divinity, compared to presenting them with a different image of God. Almost every child is more drawn to their mother than to their father. Therefore, transitioning from their earthly mother to the Heavenly Mother is very easy. The child's love for their earthly mother assists in this. Therefore, let us guide our children to the Divine Mother, who is always ready to bestow her grace upon those who worship her. I recommend this because the connection with the Divine Mother is more accessible than any other aspect of God. Sri Ramakrishna also taught this, and those who follow my advice will soon be convinced of its truth. The grace of the Divine Mother is so great that even a sinful person will be heard by her almost immediately if they fervently turn to her.

Instilling gratitude toward the Creator in children from a young age is also advantageous. Please encourage them to give thanks for everything they have, whether it be the joy of a flower, a butterfly, or a toy. Teach them to be grateful to the Lord for all these things. Every person, including children, should be thankful for food, clothing, shelter, and everything they possess because all of these things are loaned to us by God and ultimately belong to Him, not to us. They have been given to us so that we may use them for our needs or joys, as God desires us to rejoice in the things and beings we love and that He has bestowed upon us.

The mistaken belief of some people that God desires human beings to be serious and silent at all times and that one should be a bitter creature who views every human joy as something petty and false should be dismissed. Let such foolish individuals hold on to their outdated views, which only poison their own lives with their backwardness. On the contrary, God wishes us to have a cheerful mind, to enjoy and rejoice. Let the great example of Sri Ramakrishna, the great Bhakta, who laughed, joked, and performed jests with his disciples, be our guide. Even a holy person does not have to be morose. They can be very playful and cheerful, and the theosophical tales of strict "mahatmas" who do not know how to smile have been surpassed by more reliable accounts of true Masters.

By the age of seven, more can be explained to the child. This is the perfect time to explain to the child that God is the highest and only truth, that this truth can only be attained through union with God, and that the means to achieve this is through the repetition of God's name in mind with undivided attention or through the visualization of God in the mystical heart, which is located in the center of the chest.

It is also necessary to tell a seven-year-old child that God is the highest power present in everything and that this power manifests in various ways in all creatures. The highest manifestation of God is in human beings. God, as the supreme power, takes on every form in the visible and invisible nature, and this divine power is indestructible, while its forms are perishable. A piece of wood contains a portion of the divine power. If we burn the wood, the form disappears, but the divine power itself is not destroyed; it transforms into other forms like smoke and ash.

Explain to the seven-year-old child that divine power has existed in the universe for ages, and its presence in everything is what we call life. If this divine power were to cease for even a fraction of a second, everything would perish because life would have escaped from everything.

God is hidden in every living and non-living thing. All physical forces are merely transformations of this divine power that we call life. Nothing is dead; it only appears so to us when we think something has been killed or destroyed. In reality, it has simply transformed into different forms that may not be visible to our physical eyes.

# Chapter II

**God and Human Beings**

A crucial lesson for a child is understanding the relationship between God and human beings. Children are taught early on in school about the creation of the world and humans, and this poses significant challenges in providing them with the correct understanding of this biblical teaching.

It is necessary to explain to the child that science, including religious knowledge, is often misguided because it judges the Bible based on human reason and not divine wisdom.

Here we need to delve deeper into occult teachings and convey the following truths to the child: "Since the beginning of the world, there have been holy people on Earth, individuals who were initiated into divine truths. They are called prophets in the Bible because they prophesied or predicted future events that actually came true. Only those who can see into the future can be true prophets. A person who has connected with God and in whom God speaks is a prophet or Master. Many Christian saints were also prophets because they saw God, and God spoke to them.

These prophets left us what is called 'sacred books,' including the Bible. These sacred books are also known as 'divine revelations' because God revealed many of His mysteries in them. However, besides the Bible, there are other sacred books that contain much more about divine truths than the Bible. The foremost among them is an ancient Indian book called the 'Song of God' (Bhagavad Gita).

Most of these sacred books are written in cryptic language, meaning their content has multiple meanings that not everyone can understand. This is done to keep the teachings hidden from those who might misuse or disrespect them, as they are not yet ready to comprehend the hidden truth. Therefore, the

Bible can be interpreted in various ways. But the highest interpretation is spiritual, and only those who have awakened the divine spark (the Spirit of God) within them can understand it. It is only then that a person is endowed with higher insight beyond ordinary human reasoning. Our ordinary external reason can never comprehend the divine mysteries contained in the Bible and other sacred books. However, the churches only know how to interpret them according to human reason because their theologians, who interpret the Bible, have not yet received that higher wisdom (spiritual enlightenment) that one attains when one truly embarks on the Path to God. But this Path of learning is unknown to theologians because it is hidden.

On the other hand, other learned individuals, namely the Masters of mysticism and esoteric teachings, have found this Path in the words of Christ and other sacred books, especially those of India. They have revealed this Path to all people of goodwill. Thus, a secret church, or the hidden church of Christ, emerged, which is not recognized by the external churches. All the preachers of this secret, great, and solely holy Path were declared heretics and apostates by the churches, and many were imprisoned by the Catholic Church. Even secular authorities in ancient times persecuted members of the hidden church (mystics), and some were tortured and even burned at the stake."

The primary sacred book about this secret Path to God, as mentioned before, is the Indian "Song of God" (Bhagavad Gita). It is an incredibly ancient book, and nowhere is God and the Path to Him explained as clearly as in this book.

(On this occasion, it is possible to read to children from the age of seven some excerpts from the Bhagavad Gita, for example, the magnificent Chapter IX about the true knowledge of the royal secret, the divine secret.)

Then we continue: "All nations of the world, from ancient times, knew the one and true God. Anyone who claims that they were pagans is mistaken because they do not know that God has many forms and many names, and it is always the same God but under different names and forms. Therefore, all true religions in the world lead to this one God, but only if a person follows their secret or hidden teachings. No religion is without a secret Path to God, but this Path has always been known only to particularly pious individuals while it remained hidden from others. However, in our Christian religion, this Path is shown so clearly and perfectly by Jesus Christ, as it has not been shown in any other religion. Christ descended to Earth and incarnated precisely to reveal this hidden Path through His life so that everyone could find the Path with complete certainty. But even so, this Path was later misunderstood, and what the early Christians knew and understood was forgotten, and only the shell of Christ's teachings remained with the core lost. Instead, the churches replaced this Path, which you will also tread one day, with external rituals.

Those who seek God are like travelers who start from the valley below the mountains and claim to see the whole landscape from down there. Similarly, it is with people who teach religion without having seen God. They speak of God only based on hearsay or books, but not from personal experience."

However, those who begin to ascend the mountain always see further and further, and when they reach the summit, they truly behold the absolute beauty of the landscape all the way to the horizon. And these pilgrims who have climbed the mountain can provide the only true testimony of what they have seen.

Seekers on the secret Path to God gain profound insights into divine mysteries through personal experiences. As they progress and attain mastery, even reaching the state of prophets, their firsthand encounters with God enable them to become authentic religious teachers. With their personal understanding, they possess the ability to offer accurate guidance and directly illuminate the Path for others.

In the Bible and other sacred books, it is written that there have always been people who saw God and spoke with Him. It is said about Moses and all the prophets. Similarly, in foreign sacred books, there is mention everywhere of these Masters who spoke with God and saw Him. Such Masters also existed in Europe during the Middle Ages, and their many names and writings are known. At certain times, they formed special secret Brotherhoods, and there were hidden schools where they taught secret teachings.

Likewise, many ancient nations, such as the Greeks, Persians, Egyptians, Romans, and others, had such Masters or sages. These sages were initiated into secret teachings and had their famous schools. They were great saints, just like the biblical prophets, and many of them performed miraculous deeds, like Moses and others.

Those who follow the direct Path to God develop special mental powers that other people have no idea about, and such individuals often become, unintentionally, true magicians because the whole of nature is subject to them, and they can accomplish whatever they imagine.

But no Master uses these high powers to perform miracles without a purpose. They only do so when they receive a command from God. They either use these powers to help people, for example, by healing the sick, or they perform miracles to lead people to true faith in God.

However, there are other magicians who have acquired psychic powers in a different way, and they often misuse these powers for their own benefit. Some even subject certain invisible beings, who are often of evil nature, and force them to serve them. Such magicians should be avoided, and one should have nothing to do with them because they can lead others astray with their magic.

(Teaching these concepts to children is necessary. Once a child has embarked on the mystical Path, it is possible that their inner senses may open, and under certain circumstances, they may even catch a glimpse of a magician in the astral plane who could lure the child into their school. It is important to know that such false magical schools have always existed and still do. While the child, in their innocence, is protected by God after embarking on the mystical Path, it is still possible for black magicians to try anything. Therefore, I am bringing this to your attention. Besides, the child will surely share their visions with their parents, and if any suspicious being appears more frequently, we can repel it through concentration and prayer. However, there is no need to fear that astral beings or spirits would manifest to the child because they are perfectly protected against it, and such encounters do not occur on the mystical Path until the very end when the whole invisible world opens up. But by that time, everyone is already united with their God and fortified against any fear. Those who enter the mystical Path come into momentary contact, through vision, with various leaders of other schools. Occasionally, even a black magician may appear, but, like everyone else, they must be resolutely rejected through concentration on our inner divinity. That is why I touch upon these matters.)

It is essential to make the child understand that they should respect the name of God, including the names of all gods, whether old or new. This can be done mainly because we can rely on biblical commandments that state, "You shall not take the name of the Lord your God in vain." However, this commandment has another meaning related to the directive not to utter the names of God (Yahweh or Jehovah) but to only think them internally (refer to "The Fiery Bush, Part I: Mantric Exercises"). We will leave this for a later time when the child is ready.

Let us teach the child that the name of God possesses an extraordinary protective power, as well as many other powers and that the child should not utter it disrespectfully because it is the most sacred.

Regarding the relationship between human beings and God, it is necessary to explain to the child at least the most essential aspects. Tell the child something like this:

"God is eternal love, and that is why God is born within people to rejoice in their love for Him when people seek and find Him and when they unite with Him. However, God also incarnates among people on Earth in a different way. When morality declines among people, and God sees that humanity needs a new impulse to return to true faith and religion, He shows mercy to people and incarnates and appears on Earth as a human being. The most recent incarnation of God was Jesus Christ. But there were many other incarnations on Earth before Christ. They are known in India, and Indian scriptures narrate their stories.)

Similarly, in future times, it is inevitable that a new Savior will come into the world when the power of God recognizes it as necessary. Each such new Savior will always bring a new, easier Path to God for humanity and establish a new religion, a new spiritual teaching that will then spread.

If the parents are members of a particular church, they can and should instill respect for that church in their child because it serves as an external foundation for the true spiritual inner life. If the parents do not belong to any church, it is necessary for them to teach their children pure spiritual teachings based on good occult and mystical writings, the selection of which is provided on the back cover of our mystical magazine "Psyche." However, it is important to choose books wisely, and for those who are not familiar with occult literature, it is best to first inquire in writing at the "Psyche" editorial office about which books they should acquire.

# Chapter III

**About The Soul**

Before we start explaining to parents how to talk to their children about the human soul, it is necessary to give them some guidance on the questions that children will undoubtedly ask when we explain the basics of occult and mystical teachings.

A child may ask us, "And how do you know all of this?"

We can briefly answer that we know all of this from books, and the child will be satisfied for a moment, but they will continue to ponder and surprise us with further questions.

Therefore, it is necessary to satisfy the child's curiosity and thirst for knowledge at once. We can respond as follows:

"Spiritual or esoteric teachings have been revealed by God Himself to various prophets or Masters at different times, and they wrote them down in books. I have already told you that all nations have their sacred books, including the Christian Bible. But the Divine Spirit continually spreads His wisdom and imparts it either through inspiration or directly through His voice. All Masters received specific knowledge from God, which they either wrote down or passed on to their disciples. Each Master is like your schoolteacher, but their school is concerned only with spiritual matters. And when the disciples, guided by the instructions given to them by the Master, come to know God themselves, they receive further teachings directly from God, which they then write down or pass on to others. In this way, secret teachings have emerged and are scattered throughout many books in the world.

It has also happened that the teachings of the ancient prophets were preserved by the Jews in the Bible. Then Jesus Christ came and brought new teachings, followed by other lesser Masters who brought more and more new insights about God, for God is infinite, and humanity will never fully comprehend Him.

Therefore, the teachings about God are eternal and infinite.

The ancient sages of other nations have also left us their accounts of God and the Path to Him, and all of this is now summarized in mystical teachings, which means hidden teachings. One Master passed on this teaching to another until it reached our time, a process that took thousands of years. The last one was a certain Kerning, who wrote many beautiful books about this secret Path. And it is from him that the author of this book received this teaching.

The Holy Spirit always finds someone who will heed His voice and become a disseminator of His teachings. That is how this teaching has reached our Czech books, from which we are instructing you."

A lot depends on always telling children the whole truth and avoiding evasive answers because children instinctively sense when they have not been answered sincerely.

Regarding the soul, it is necessary to tell the child the following:

"The human soul is the most precious treasure a person has. It has embodied itself in this body only to diligently seek God, who dwells within it and whose abode the soul is. And conversely, our body is the abode of the soul and must, therefore, be cared for, nourished, and kept as clean as possible to avoid defilement. However, if the body has been defiled in some way, a person must sincerely repent their mistakes and ask God within themselves for forgiveness."

Furthermore, it is necessary to explain to the child that the soul is eternal and continues to exist even after the death of the body. When a person dies, the soul leaves the body and continues its existence on another level of being. Some religions refer to this as the afterlife or life after death. The soul can then be reborn into a new body and undergo further life, which is called reincarnation.

It is important to explain to the child that the purpose of the soul is to go through various life experiences, learn, and spiritually grow. The soul goes through different life lessons and carries its karma, which is the consequence of its past actions, into new lives. Each life is an opportunity for the soul to learn something new, develop spiritually, and fulfill its purpose.

Children should be encouraged to understand that their souls are on a journey of growth and evolution and that their actions and choices have an impact on their spiritual development. It is important to teach them the values of kindness, compassion, honesty, and love, as these qualities contribute to the growth of their souls.

Moreover, it is essential to emphasize to children that they have the potential to connect with their inner divine nature and develop a personal relationship with God. They can do this through prayer, meditation, and living a virtuous life aligned with spiritual principles.

It is crucial to answer children's questions about the soul with patience, simplicity, and honesty, tailoring the explanations to their age and level of understanding. Encouraging their curiosity and providing them with a solid foundation of spiritual knowledge will support their spiritual growth and help them navigate their own spiritual journey.

The soul is of a fiery nature, as it is a reflection of God, who is also a living fire, though not like the fire we see on Earth. This divine fire is millions of times purer and entirely colorless. This fire of God manifests to those who truly serve God, not just through religious rituals and ceremonies but through inner prayer. I will tell you more about this inner prayer, which is extremely powerful, later.

A person has an outer soul and an inner soul. What you think in your mind is not your true soul but rather the earthly soul, which dissipates after the death of the body, just as the body disintegrates in the grave. However, the dissipation of the soul can sometimes take a very long time. On the other hand, the true soul, the heavenly soul, which remains hidden within a person, is immortal and is a part of God who dwells within it. When a person embarks on the secret Path to God, this soul reveals itself to them as the Virgin Mary or as another goddess.

Therefore, we must hold the name of the Virgin Mary and all goddesses, even those considered pagan, in the highest respect. The Virgin Mary, who gave birth to Jesus Christ, is not the same as the inner Virgin. She was a physical woman, but one who had attained a high level of mastery and prophecy and was chosen by God to become the mother of our Savior.

The teachings about this inner Virgin are secret, and current religious institutions have no knowledge of them. However, anyone who honors the Virgin Mary, the mother of Jesus, unknowingly honors the inner sacred Virgin—the soul—who always accepts this reverence.

The heavenly soul continually incarnates into new bodies, so each one of us has been on Earth many times as a human, always in a different body. We have had different names, different parents, and perhaps a different country of birth. The heavenly soul repeats these incarnations according to God's law in order to save and guide the human soul toward God. This is known as salvation or entering the kingdom of heaven.

Our human soul, which we refer to as "our self," is mortal and not immortal, as commonly taught. One part of our soul is directed upwards toward the heavenly soul, while the other part is inclined toward the body and its desires. Within the body, there is another part of a person that leans toward evil and negative things. This part also disintegrates and breaks apart after death. Those who excessively indulge in material pleasures such as food, drink, and other unnecessary things and who never think about their heavenly soul or their inner God wander and suffer in the invisible world that surrounds us after death. Their lower soul is obscured and often shrouded in darkness, and they must sometimes wait for many years before dissipation. We help these suffering souls of the departed through prayer, which facilitates their dissipation and reduces their torment.

This lower soul carries all its earthly desires into the invisible world. The drunkard suffers from an unquenchable thirst, the glutton always feels hungry, and the miser is constantly afraid of the earthly treasures that they have had to leave behind. However, the worst suffering in the invisible world is experienced by criminals and suicides because they acted against the supreme law of God, either against love for others or by not preserving and caring for their bodies to fulfill their role, which is to come closer to God as much as possible.

But a person can only fulfill this role while they are on Earth. Once they die, they cannot further progress because they disintegrate into their invisible components. Then their souls must wait until they are reincarnated again.

Therefore, we must protect and care for our bodies, not for worldly pleasures and indulgences, but to make them suitable instruments for God. However, we know nothing about our past lives on Earth because the center of our knowledge was in the physical human brain, which disintegrates after death, and the part we call the human soul dissipates. In each life, we receive a new body and, consequently, a new brain in which nothing remains from our previous life.

However, a Master who has reached God remembers all their past lives very clearly and knows the path they walked for thousands of years before realizing God.

Just as divinity is present in humans, it is also present in everything else, in the living and the non-living. God is present in all plants and animals, and in every creature, it manifests differently according to the level of its perfection. Everything originated from God in ancient times, and everything must return to God when everything is perfected so that everything will know God.

If we want to physically illustrate spiritual principles to a child, we can do so quite easily with two mirrors. We light a candle or a lamp and explain that its flame, or light, is an image of God. Then we show the child the reflection of that flame in the first mirror and tell them that it is the reflected light and that the flame in the mirror is an image of the heavenly soul, which directly receives the light of reason and higher wisdom from God. We then take the second mirror and reflect the image of the flame from the first mirror, explaining that it represents the human conscience, which resides in the human soul. We show that this light is much dimmer than the flame of a candle or lamp. Yet, even this reflection in the second mirror can, to some extent, comprehend God metaphorically. When we take a sheet of paper and place it in the shadow and reflect the light of the candle from the second mirror onto it, we see a faint gleam, which is an image of weak human reason that believes it comprehends everything while being limited and dark. Nevertheless, this small human reason has devised so many things and made so many inventions with God's permission.

(On this occasion, we can suggest to the child that it is wrong to attach too much importance to human inventions, especially technical ones. We must confront the current tendency, particularly in the daily press, to celebrate technology, which is essentially a temptation to make humans vain about their own achievements, neglecting the works of God, namely nature.)

We can say the following to a child about conscience:

"Conscience is the secret voice of God. When we turn inward to our conscience, we receive inspiration from God, namely secret thoughts that rightly guide us, like a bright beam of a lantern on a path in the deep forest at night. We must not silence our conscience with indifference but always follow its instructions. Conscience is the only thread that still connects ordinary people to God. Otherwise, people are entirely without God and are worse off than animals, which always obey the laws of nature, which are the same as the laws of God. Although, according to human understanding, animals commit evil deeds (like predatory animals), they still do not act against the laws of God because they do nothing out of malice or enmity. They only defend themselves or listen to their instincts to satisfy their needs. However, humans, who have been given reason and also the higher gift from God, which is conscience, must not harm their fellow beings. If they do, they commit a decline that God's law punishes with suffering, which always follows. God Himself never punishes anyone because He is eternal love and cannot punish. However, God allows various trials to befall individuals or even entire nations to purify humanity through them and to make progress. Often, God also tests His greatest favorites (saints) in this way and sends them trials to see if they remain devoted to Him and if their faith is strengthened. But when such people have overcome everything and have not turned away from God or complained against Him, He rewards them greatly and finally grants them eternal bliss and unlimited power, as we mentioned at the beginning, that all prophets and Masters possess. In a person who truly follows the secret Path to God, conscience will ultimately develop into an authentic voice of God, which is absolutely clear and always infallible.

Whoever has this voice of God, which is called the inner Word, is a prophet and can learn all earthly and heavenly mysteries. That is the goal of each of us, and when we achieve it, we no longer need any books or earthly teachers because our Teacher has become our inner God, who is also called the inner highest Master or Jesus Christ.

Just as biblical Jesus Christ was born in Bethlehem in a stable, in every person, Jesus Christ is born as their personal inner divinity. And he is also born in a stable, which is an image of the human body, which is of animal nature.

We must explain to the child that conscience is a divine gift that guides us toward goodness, love, and compassion. It is the voice of God within us, helping us distinguish between right and wrong. By following our conscience, we align ourselves with God's will and experience inner peace and harmony.

Furthermore, we can emphasize to the child the importance of nurturing and cultivating their inner connection with God. This can be achieved through prayer, meditation, and acts of kindness and love toward others. By developing a strong relationship with their inner divinity, they can experience spiritual growth and find guidance and strength in their journey through life.

It's essential to encourage the child to listen to their conscience and follow its guidance. By doing so, they can develop a deep sense of integrity, moral values, and empathy toward others. They will understand that their actions have consequences and that their choices should always be aligned with the principles of love, compassion, and justice.

Overall, teaching a child about the spiritual aspects of life should be done with simplicity, honesty, and respect for their level of understanding. It is a gradual process that requires patience and continuous guidance, allowing them to explore and develop their own spiritual connection in a way that is meaningful to them.

Therefore, a person is externally like an animal with their body, but internally they have a divine origin. However, one can only attain this God through the secret Path, which involves a specific mode of thinking that I will explain later.

Jesus Christ, just like Virgin Mary, has a dual nature. All sacred Scriptures have multiple meanings, including a historical interpretation, such as the known details of Christ's birth, teachings, and miracles. This is the historical explanation. Then there is the secret interpretation, which reveals that Christ is the Lord of the entire universe, governing it with divine power from the invisible Sun, which is beyond our visible sun. This is why ancient civilizations worshipped the sun, essentially worshipping God, who resides beyond our sun.

Jesus Christ has incarnated many times on Earth to teach humanity the true religion, appearing under different names in different countries throughout millennia. He will come again in the future, and at that time, many people will be saved and brought into the kingdom of God. It is said that this time is approaching, and therefore, everyone should prepare for the coming of the next Jesus Christ, who could even be unexpected.

Furthermore, the Holy Spirit, which resides as a flame or spark in the spiritual heart of every person, is also known as Jesus Christ. The exact name is not crucial, as we can refer to our inner God as the Holy Spirit.

However, each person can adapt these teachings according to their understanding. I advise parents to not overwhelm their children with too much information at once. Sometimes, it's better to share only a part or provide hints. Children naturally show a particular interest in new and mysterious things.

Some children may resist these teachings, but it is not the parents' fault. Such a child may have been sent to their family as a test. It is also possible that the inclination toward religious and mystical matters will only appear in such a child later. Therefore, one should not despair if faced with difficulties.

However, in most cases, it can be expected that souls who have already encountered the mystical Path or have some knowledge of the secret teachings will be sent to families of mystics. It is a natural law that the Path is made easier for these souls by being born into mystic parents. Conversely, it is also possible for souls lost in ignorance and darkness to appear in such families, as they can gain the first rays of light from them. In such cases, we must be patient and do our best to save the soul of our child from the snares of this world.

Sometimes, a backward child may be a karmic punishment. In such cases, we must guide and restrain them as much as possible. Just as not every adult is suited for mysticism, not every child will be interested in these matters. We must not impose occult and, especially, mystical teachings on such a child. It is true that no seed sown is ever lost, but in many cases, its strength and growth remain hidden and will bear fruit in a future existence.

However, if a child shows early interest, especially if they ask questions willingly, we can rejoice, as they are likely to embark on the Path at the right time.

# Chapter IV

**Reincarnation and Karma**

From the very beginning of teaching our children, it is necessary to slowly and cautiously introduce them to the correct occult laws that govern the entire universe. One of these laws is reincarnation, which refers to the repeated embodiment of the human soul into human bodies until the soul overcomes matter, meaning the body, and attains salvation. However, as we know, salvation is the return to the spiritual or heavenly state, in other words, the return to God.

Since every Christian child is taught biblical history, we can rely on this fact and present the true essence of the lives of the first humans in the Garden of Eden based on the occult experiences of ancient Masters.

Adam and Eve are merely prototypes or examples of the first humans, as there were more of them than described in the Bible. These first humans had bodies that were completely different from ours; they were spiritual bodies, invisible to us in our current state. The first humans saw God and spoke with Him at any time, as described in the Bible. They lived in harmony with nature, which is why even shy and wild animals behaved friendly toward humans, not only without fear but also without posing any threat.

The first humans understood the language of all animals; they knew not only the names of animals but also the names of plants and everything in the world because they possessed natural magical senses. They saw the essence of every object and had command over all natural forces. They controlled the elements, and their mystical abilities were immeasurable. In ancient Kabbalistic writings, it is mentioned that Adam could see from one end of the world to the other, signifying his absolute clairvoyance.

However, these human souls, the first humans, fell deeply into the matter of this heavenly state. As a result, they acquired gross physical bodies like ours, and matter simultaneously overshadowed their higher senses. They forgot their origin, lost their magical and spiritual powers, and eventually even forgot about God because they could no longer see or hear Him.

However, as mentioned before, the human soul did not lose its inner treasure, its eternal essence. In every human soul, there is a divine spark, the entire unmanifested God, the same God that exists in the universe. However, humans are unaware of this God; they do not know Him and have no knowledge of Him. Occasionally, they may have a faint sense that this most tremendous power in the universe is hidden within them, but it remains dormant. Only a few individuals are bestowed with the great grace of recognizing this power within themselves. The majority of people need to be taught these truths by more advanced individuals and have this truth revealed to them.

For the human soul to be able to return to God, it must continually reincarnate on Earth or other worlds into physical bodies. During this process, the soul continuously evolves, expanding its perspective and clarifying its inner feelings until it reaches such perfection that it recognizes its inner God. By doing so, it achieves personal immortality and is saved for eternity. This is when the soul enters paradise, a blissful state it was in before its fall.

It is essential to explain to the child that paradise is not a specific place on Earth but a spiritual state where the soul can exist anywhere without changing this state. Therefore, all great prophets or Masters attained the same knowledge, abilities, and powers as Adam and Eve. We can read about this in the sacred texts of all nations.

Regarding the duration of the interim period between two incarnations, we can tell the child that this period is not always the same. Sometimes it can last several hundred or even thousands of years, while in spiritually advanced individuals who have embarked on the mystical Path, the path to God, this interval between two human existences can be as short as a year, several months, or even just a few days.

The second important question is the law of karma. It is crucial to teach the child about karma early on because knowing this law can prevent them from easily falling into depressive or desperate moods, which primarily occurs today, where even twelve-year-old children sometimes resort to suicide out of despair.

The law of karma is simultaneously the law of divine Justice. Every individual sows seeds of both good and evil in each incarnation on Earth. These seeds are their actions, thoughts, and words. Every action, every thought, and every spoken word affects the law of retribution because all these things bear their consequences, usually in a subsequent earthly life. Those who have performed many good deeds in one of their lives, or even those who only desired to perform them but were unable to, have generated good karma. This good karma must manifest itself beneficially in future existences, resulting in a life filled with good rewards.

Similarly, the same applies to adverse actions, thoughts, and words. Every person experiences the consequences in their current existence for the evil deeds they committed, the evil thoughts they had, or the evil words they spoke in a past existence. However, parents should know that karma does not always fully manifest in the following existence. There are specific laws known only to the highest Masters, according to which the fruits of one's actions, even from several past lives, manifest in a particular existence, while the rest of the consequences remain hidden and may appear later.

Sometimes, a portion of karma is resolved in the same existence where the actions occurred, while the other part awaits the next or subsequent lives. Yogis refer to this hidden part of karma as "latent karma." This latent karma can be forgiven. This is the meaning behind the words of Christ in the Lord's Prayer: "Forgive us our sins!"

Mystics know that karma can be dissolved entirely through mystical exercises, that is, by the grace of God. Otherwise, karma must be fully experienced to its last consequence.

Therefore, it is advisable to teach children about these laws of eternal retribution from the very beginning. It is not God who punishes or rewards anyone, but rather, it is the law of nature itself. God does not punish or reward; individuals punish or reward themselves based on how they live. It is as if we threw a stone directly above us and let it fall on our heads. We punish ourselves through our own ignorance, and it is this ignorance that leads us to commit evil deeds, the fruits of which return to us.

If children were taught these crucial principles from a young age, drawn from the ancient teachings of Indian sages, the world would soon be different from what it is now. Everyone would have reverence for the law of karma, knowing that they punish themselves for their wrong actions and that the consequences of these evil deeds cannot be avoided.

Everyone must also recognize that the teaching of the law of karma itself is much higher and purer than the religious doctrine of a punishing God. Such a concept of God distorts our understanding of the infinite and boundless greatness of God and makes Him similar to imperfect human beings.

As today's modern children are much more intelligent than in the past, they will easily grasp these spiritual laws. If instilled in them from an early age, their souls will accept and be guided by these laws throughout their lives.

# Chapter V

**On Prayer and The First Exercise**

It is necessary to awaken the child's interest in spiritual matters. Every child, regardless of gender, has a desire to discover unknown things, and the more distant these things are, the deeper the curiosity. Children often ask questions about stars, their distance, their quantity, their names, whether there are people living there, and so on. These questions are closely related to occult and spiritual teachings. They can easily be connected to the infinity of the universe, which is a prerequisite for the infinity of God. If the universe were finite, as some faithless scientists, such as Einstein, try to prove, then God would also be finite and not God.

Therefore, any such question a child asks about the universe can easily be transformed into thoughts about God, His infinity, omnipotence, and omnipresence. The divine omnipresence is important because we can tell the child, for example, "God is present in everything and everywhere. He is present in every mineral, every flower, every little animal, in streams, rivers, and seas, in the depths of the earth, in the clouds, and in the heavens, in all the stars. He is also present in every human being and resides in the so-called mystical heart, which is in the center of the chest."

When we teach children in this way, we can show them the place where they have their inner God. There is the sanctuary, the inner temple, and it is there that every prayer and every request to God should be directed! And since this God is present in everyone, we are all brothers and sisters and should not harm anyone because by doing so, we harm ourselves.

I have already mentioned that it is necessary to teach children to turn their minds inward, into the mystical heart, during prayer, instead of directing their thoughts somewhere above the clouds because our divinity is closest to us in our own hearts. In this context, we can also explain to the child the mysterious secret that God knows and sees everything and hears what we do, say, and think. It is precisely this divinity within us that constantly guides, directs, and watches over us, and nothing can escape its gaze. And since this divinity within us is identical to God, who is present throughout the entire universe, of which we are a part, we actually, without realizing it, live in God, for God is life itself. Without God, we would not live for even a single second.

It is very important to teach the child to pray with a sense of respect and fervor and not just recite prayers with empty words while thinking about something else. We need to awaken in the child an early interest in mystical experiences, in high spiritual powers that are hidden within us. This can be achieved with even the youngest children through fairy tales or by reading stories of miracles about saints, yogis, and masters.

In this regard, I recommend the book *Divy a kouzla indických fakirů* (Miracles and Wonders of Indian Fakirs). However, it is necessary to make a careful selection from this book and retell the stories in our own words. It is also essential to explain these fairy tales in a factual manner and according to occult truths. Children are often very interested in stories about fairies and gnomes. We should not make them believe in these beings because, in doing so, we would also take away their belief in higher spiritual beings and the world of the spirit in general. Instead, let us teach children that these invisible beings often serve good and pious people, helping them achieve earthly and spiritual wealth.

Many children, in their early years, see the invisible world, not only various natural spirits but also astral beings. Many children up to the age of three interact with an invisible entity during the day and play with it during the night. With such children, it is necessary to carefully observe their further development as they possess psychic abilities that usually fade away after the third year, causing the child to forget these significant experiences as they grow older. However, we should remember that every such child already carries the seed of a future mystical journey within them, and therefore, we should never neglect them in this regard.

Furthermore, through cautious questioning, we can help preserve this psychic ability in the child until the age when they can speak coherently and describe the scenes they have witnessed.

It is crucial to instill in children from the very beginning the true and proper concepts of God. What churches present to people about God is inadequate and fragmented. The ancient Indians, in their sacred scriptures, better explained the essence of God. The most important of such scriptures are the Bhagavad Gita and the Vedas, as well as the Upanishads, which are Persian extracts from the ancient Vedas. However, it is challenging to find suitable passages in an extensive book like the Bhagavad Gita to share with children.

Although the Bhagavad Gita is very comprehensible and straightforward, it is also vast, and it contains profound philosophical ideas that a child cannot yet grasp. The Vedas and Upanishads are inaccessible to most people, and moreover, they are extensive in their content, making it difficult for the average reader to find specific passages. Additionally, the Bhagavad Gita is currently unavailable, and it is uncertain when a new edition will be released. Therefore, I present here a few excerpts from the "Addenda" that I have included in my translation of the Bhagavad Gita. This addendum is translated directly from the Jedi Veda and the Upanishads. The following sentences can be adapted by parents to simplify them further and teach children about God, His existence, and His attributes.

*Paraatma and Dživatma both exist from the beginning.*

*Paraatma is the knowledge of the whole, and Dživatma is the knowledge of the individual.*

*Paraatma possesses free will, but Dživatma does not. And Maya, which is the attribute of Brahman's will, is enduring in terms of the past and impermanent in terms of the future, providing enjoyment to all beings.*

Explanation: Paraatma is the manifested God, the universal God. Dživatma is the personal divinity within every being, including humans. Therefore, Paraatma has free will, while Dživatma does not, as human will is limited. Maya is nature with all its forces and manifestations; it is the garment of God, thrown into visible space by the will of Brahman, the hidden and unmanifested God.

Thus, Maya is enduring in the past but not in the future because Maya, encompassing all visible worlds, must eventually perish and return to the womb of Brahman. Maya binds us through our five senses, connecting us to the manifested material world and granting us earthly life. Therefore, one who overcomes all five senses through the mystical path will unveil the divine and behold God. This veil, precisely, is Maya.

*"A Paraatma is endless, and the whole world is his form. Although the entire world is his form, he is not active in any way."*

Explanation: The entire world takes the form of the manifested God, as known by the ancient Kabbalists who referred to this form as Adam Kadmon. It is a human form. Thus, it is stated in the Bible that God created man in his own image. The garment of God is the universe, and this garment takes the form of the human body. However, Paraatma remains in absolute stillness, for according to our understanding, he does nothing now, as his activity was only present in the single moment when the entire world radiated from him. A more detailed explanation of this apparent mystery, which belongs to the mysteries of

God, can be found by readers in my translation of Master Eckhart, published by the "Psyche" society.

*"Maya is limited and subject to destruction, but Dživatma is free and imperishable, and Dživatma destroys Maya by the power of knowledge. Above Maya, which is subject to destruction, and above Dživatma, which is not subject to destruction, there is the luminous being of the Lord."*

Explanation: Nature is limited and bound to perish eventually. However, the divine soul within a human being is free and eternal. Through the mystical path of self-realization, one can transcend the influence of Maya (illusion) and realize their own divine nature. Above the divine soul and Maya, there exists the unmanifested divine essence characterized by light. The process of this transformation is further elucidated in the teachings.

*"Whoever realizes this and unites with it becomes the master of oneself, destroys visible existence, transcends the bondage of Maya, and attains knowledge of that luminous being. By freeing oneself from the entanglements and bonds of ignorance, ego, will, enmity, and*

*fear, one attains salvation from rebirth in other worlds and from death. And because they have realized the all-embracing and singular Existence, have liberated themselves from heaven and hell, have seen all their desires fulfilled in this world, and have gained mastery over the entire world, they remain in the third world, which is the world of being."*

Explanation: First and foremost, it is necessary to realize this truth and then have unwavering faith in it as the ultimate truth. Then, one can embark on the path guided by this truth, leading to the luminous being. Along this path, a person gains self-mastery, destroys their visible existence, which includes the physical and astral bodies, and breaks free from the bonds of nature or Maya. They become liberated, free from ignorance, fear, and enmity, and overcome the fear of death, as they no longer need to reincarnate or experience death. The statement about liberation from heaven and hell imply that the enlightened individual, having realized the divine within themselves, transcends astral realms and attains divine powers. Every desire of such an individual is fulfilled in this world, and they become the master of the entire world, residing in the third world, which is the divine world.

Now I come to the most crucial part of these quotes:

*"In the depths of every body and every soul resides this luminous Being, which knows hidden mysteries, is eternal and is both knowable and unknowable, and besides it, there is no other existence."*

Explanation: The luminous being of God resides in everything, including every creature and human being. In humans, it dwells in the mystical heart, which is located in the middle of the chest. Within this luminous being of God, the key to all mysteries is stored. It can be known through the mystical path, but it remains unknowable to all others. It represents the true existence, while everything else is non-existent and an illusion of nature or Maya.

*"The way of true repentance and knowledge is this: To know the truth of all truths, restrain the senses like the sun and hold the heart with a firm rein. And when the light, which is the natural warmth of the entire world, enters its sphere, it illuminates the entire atmosphere*

*with this light. As a blessing for this repentance, which it first accomplished before all others, the sun attains its greatness."*

Explanation: The restraining of the senses and holding the heart with a firm rein, as mentioned in the quote, refers to a state of quiet concentration and envisioning a small sun in the spiritual heart. This represents the act of repentance, leading to knowledge and realization. Restraining the senses means withdrawing from sensory perceptions; holding the heart refers to controlling one's thoughts. The sun is a visible symbol of God and is the best symbol that can be formed through focused concentration. The sun is considered the abode of all Saviors, including Jesus Christ. The reference to the Savior's repentance in this sentence signifies their descent to Earth as an example for all humanity and to achieve greatness.

*"From this reason, the ancient nations worshipped Him; there is nothing left for them to do, for He has become the One. So when a person makes their own torch the light of Dživatma and recognizes the pure Brahman, they are saved by it."*

Explanation: The human soul is veiled by ignorance like a crystal covered in mud. But those practicing yoga or mysticism wash away this ignorance, and their spirit merges with God, becoming God itself and radiating just like divinity. One whose inner light becomes their lantern has accomplished their task, for they have united with God. Now I will mention some essential qualities of God as described in the ancient sacred texts of India. These are very important because they lead us to a more correct understanding of God and divert us from incorrect religious notions. Almost all present-day religions describe God too anthropomorphically or, as scholars say, too human-like. However, this is an entirely erroneous notion that must be destroyed in the tender soul of a child and replaced with the correct concept. When we do this, we perform a great and good deed because we adjust and facilitate the child's path to God. Our most significant obstacles are our erroneous opinions, especially in occult and religious matters. But false opinions and misconceptions often hinder us even in material matters and frequently lead to losses and even ruin. However, spiritual matters are much more important because losses or even ruin in this realm have terrifying effects. Let us now hear what the Oupnek'hat says about God."

*"And that original truth was not created; it is motionless, it is independent of everything, and it is light. When people know this, they are freed from all the snares of sin."*

*"That luminous being is in all spaces, it permeates every nook and cranny and fills it, becomes predominantly visible, and is the same in the entire inner world. It is what was, what is, and what will be."*

Explanation: God is truth, and that truth was never created, and this truth is eternal light. The one who has recognized these truths is freed from the snares of sin. But even if a person only knows it, and if they follow this knowledge, they cannot commit any sin at all. This is because God, or the luminous being, is omnipresent. When it manifests to a yogi or mystic, it first becomes visible. Then its manifestations come in different ways to others.

*"Oh, people, wherever you look, you see His face! And the light that is fire is He, and the light that is in water is also He. His light has*

*entered all worlds and all plants, both large and small."*

Explanation: Let us teach children to see God in all of nature. Let us teach them to see Him in the Sun and encourage them to imagine a little sun in their hearts and focus on it! When we explain to a child that God is in the sun and that God is also in that little sun they imagine in their hearts, the child quickly understands this truth. If the child is naturally inclined toward mysticism, they will gladly concentrate on their little sun, which they will love.

At the same time, we can constantly remind the child not to forget the sun because there is true divinity within it. Just as the physical sun is the center of all life on all planets and the source of this life, the spiritual sun, which is beyond the physical sun, is the source of all spiritual life and inner enlightenment. It is necessary to explain this to children so that they see the sun as a visible sign of God, even as His throne.

The sun's image can be easily formed in the spiritual heart because it is almost visible daily, and its radiant disc is imaginable on a small scale. Therefore, whoever does this daily practice and focuses on such an image of the sun will soon receive evidence that they are on the right path.

*"Even now, everyone who repents should first utter this prayer and seek the assistance of the Sun: With the help of the sun, which is light, I achieve repentance to enter the world of Truth and be blessed! May my heart be united with true faith, may the sun be inclined toward me, and may it shine upon my path to paradise so that I may reach it, for the sun is the gate to paradise!"*

Explanation: Seeking assistance from the sun signifies seeking assistance from Jesus Christ. Those whom Christ favors will have an illuminated path to paradise, for Christ is the gateway. That is why Christ also said, "I am the door!" Through this door, we enter the spiritual world. And this can only be accomplished through Christ or His symbol, the sun.

*"The Brahmins who kept their senses strictly under control focused on the sun, and the one among them who reached the highest degree of repentance, the sun allows them, as the giver of rewards for good deeds, to reach*

*Brahma through the path of light. Therefore, the sun deserves honor and praise."*

Explanation: Here, we have it explicitly stated that in India, they focused on the sun, not the physical sun, but rather the sun within the spiritual heart.

*"The manifestation of Brahma over the soul of the yogi, who subtly enters into another state, is indicated at times by a pearl, at times by smoke, at times by the light of the sun, at times by fire, at times by the light into which the wind blows, at times by the glowworm that shines at night, at times like a flickering lightning, at times like a pure and white crystal, and at times like the light of the moon."*

Explanation: The manifestation of God occurs in every yogi and mystic through these means. Our source states that the yogi subtly enters into another state. When concentration is performed correctly, the mind enters into a subtle calmness, like the still surface of the sea, unaffected by any movement. In this state, which lies between sleep and wakefulness and serves as a boundary between the two, the mystic perceives things from the divine world, some of which are indicated here.

Just as a crystal is smeared with mud, causing its transparency to disappear, but regains its purity and luster after being washed, so the original Dživatma (divine soul), which is a luminous being, loses its light of manifestation due to the mud of ignorance. But when it is cleansed through yoga and knowledge, the spirit becomes clear and visible, the cloudiness disappears, and its actions and deeds are concluded. This is because it relied solely on the help of this divine Sun, which it possesses, to turn to it in all its childhood anxieties and worries or in fear. Therefore, let us assure the child that it is under the protection of this inner God in the form of the little sun and that this inner God never leaves them. In this way, we cultivate faith and trust in the inner divinity within the child.

In instructional books, we read and often hear from religious teachers to avoid all sins because God sees everything. But tell something similar to a child, especially a modern child. For such a child, God is a being somewhere beyond the stars, and the child, when doing something in secret, does not believe at all that God could see it. It is also natural because God is invisible, and even an adult does not have a correct conception of Him. So, where would a child get such a conception?

But suppose we tell the child that God in the form of a bit of sun is within their inner being, that He is always with them, protecting and watching over them, and therefore sees every stumble and even knows what the child is thinking in the deepest recesses of their soul. In that case, the child will understand that they can never escape from such an observer. And if we continue to instill this truth in the child's mind, it will remain in their memory and guide their actions. Let us also teach the child to bow to this little inner sun, to pray to it, and turn to it with all their needs. Let them also pray to it for the health and well-being of their parents and all their loved ones.

*"Let us bow to that luminous being! And what is singular and has nothing else, and what with its most diverse forces acts upon everything, rules over all lights and all beings, was the one before the emergence of all things. Yet, in the form of its manifestation, it remains*

*equally unique! Therefore, whoever knows this one becomes imperishable."*

The preceding sentence is clear.

*"That one and only Spirit, who also destroys everything, has no other. By its power, it overcomes all worlds and is within the innermost beings of all worlds. And on the final day, when it absorbs all worlds into itself, it will come to pass that all worlds and everything created and sustained within them will be assimilated by it."*

Explanation: Here, another aspect of God is described, which the Indians call Shiva and is known as the Destroyer. Eventually, the entire nature returns to its source, that is, to that one, with all worlds and all beings. However, this cannot happen until all beings reach the necessary height until all become the highest initiates. Therefore, every person must become a mystic at some point to know God and unite with Him.

Some may reach this state earlier and others later, but everyone must ultimately pass through the gateway of mysticism. Only in this way can one be free from the suffering that reigns throughout the universe and affects every creature until they reach God. Therefore, whoever has been shown this gateway should not hesitate and enter it.

*"In all directions is His eye, His mouth is everywhere, His hand is everywhere, and His foot is everywhere. His hands work in everything, and He gives wings to all birds to fly. And since He created the heaven and the earth, His one light is within their core. And all creatures come forth from Him and return to Him. He is the Lord of the whole world, and the entire world is His creation. He is the great knower and the truth."*

Explanation: Here, we have another figurative explanation of the attributes of God.

*"Above all, He created the Spirit that lives in human hearts. He is the only being who created the Spirit, and may He grant us the knowledge to realize that we are connected to Him."*

Explanation: Above all else, the human spirit was created, which emerged directly from the hands of God and resided in human hearts. Our spirit has the same attributes as the

Creator and the same powers. Still, as long as it is bound to Maya, or nature, within this physical body that blinds it, it cannot fully unfold these attributes. However, once a person embarks on the mystical path, these attributes begin to manifest.

*"Whoever knows Him will attain immortality after death, but apart from this path, there is no other. Besides the spirit, there is no higher being. He is like a straight and sturdy tree, and in the entire world, He is the only tree that extends across the entire world.*

*"And that which is greater than the human spirit has no essence and is universal. This universal divinity is bound to everything when this world is visible. And when the world becomes invisible (when it dissolves into Brahman), it becomes the universal spirit in everything, which knows no bodily evil."*

Explanation: The unmanifested God does not have forms and permeates the entire universe. As long as the world is visible, like it is now, this universal divinity is bound to it. However, when everything merges back into God, and the visible world dissolves, this divinity becomes the universal Spirit that transcends suffering.

*"Whoever realizes it becomes immortal — whoever does not realize it must continue to suffer."*

Explanation: By realization, it means experiencing this truth. Those who have experienced it within themselves attain immortality. Those who have not experienced it through the mystical path will continue to suffer until this truth truly manifests within them and until they have recognized their own God.

*"Every mouth is his mouth, all heads are his head, every throat is his throat. He is in the drink of all hearts of all creatures, and he embraces everything deserving of our worship. Therefore, he is the form of joy, and this form is present everywhere. He is the king of kings, who fills everything. He grants movement to all creatures and resides in the highest bliss. He is light without flaws."*

Explanation: He grants movement to all creatures, meaning life itself. For God Himself is essentially life.

*"That Purusha (Spirit) has innumerable heads and immeasurable external and internal senses. It embraces all five elements and resides in the width of ten fingers above the navel, in the chest, where the heart is."*

Explanation: Purusha is another name for the divine spirit. It resides in the human being just above the navel, within the width of ten fingers, when hands are placed flat on the body just above the navel. This place is in the middle of the chest, not in the physical but in the spiritual heart. We should focus our attention there, not on the body, but on our inner self. We must maintain the image of that little sun within that place in our mind, keeping it in constant radiance as much as possible. Once it disappears, we have ceased concentrating because we are not yet trained. After some time, we will be able to maintain this image for longer, as mentioned in The Fire of Truth, Part I. Then the connection with the inner divinity will immediately occur, manifesting in various ways. For further information, the reader is referred to the chapter on Concentration in The Fire of Truth. The matter is straightforward, yet not everyone understands it, as evidenced by thousands of written and letter questions that the author of that work must constantly answer. Those who do not understand are not yet mature for the mystical path. But those who understand can practice concentration without any further instructions or explanations. Such a person is mature for the mystical path. If our child does not understand, we must tell them to pray within themselves, meaning to that indicated place of the Supreme Lord, for grace. Once grace is received, the person, whether a child or an adult, will immediately understand. The following contains important instructions about this spirit, and they are so simple that even a child can understand them.

*"That which is visible, that which was, and that which will be is the Purusha.*
*"He bestows bliss. Through Maya (external nature), which is the manifestation of his will, he appears in various forms, and what appears as individual beings through Maya is also him. His hand, foot, and eye exist in all directions. In all directions, his head, his ear, and his mouth exist, for he permeates everything.*
*"He is the Lord above all and the teacher of all.*
*"He is the protector of all and the helper of all.*
*"The city, i.e., the human body, has nine gates. Within this city is the Jivatma, which remains*

*ever wakeful and abides in that state but is completely independent of everything."*

Explanation: The human body has nine gates, namely nine openings, including the mouth, ears, eyes, nostrils, and two openings of the excretory organs. Indians and many Western mystics refer to the human body as a 'city.' The spirit within us remains ever vigilant, as confirmed by the biblical verse: 'Neither slumbers nor sleeps the one who guards you.

*"Everything that moves and that which does not move is within its grasp."*
*"Although it has neither hands nor feet, it still comprehends everything and goes everywhere. Though it has no eyes, it sees; though it has no ears, it hears."*
*"And it knows everything; there is nothing it does not know."*
*"It pervades everything and is the origin of everything."*
*"That is why I call it the Greatest of All."*
*"It has the greatest volume, yet it is the smallest and most subtle. It resides within the depths of the heart."*

Explanation: explains the metaphor of the human body as a city with its nine gates or openings. The spirit or divine essence within us is constantly aware and attentive. The text further describes the all-encompassing nature of the spirit, its ability to perceive and comprehend without physical organs, and its infinite knowledge. It emphasizes that the spirit pervades everything and is the source of all creation. The spirit is called the Greatest of All, having immense capacity despite its subtle and profound nature, and resides within the depths of the heart.

*"But in that 'least,' because in the human body, it has the length of a human thumb, as stated in the sacred Indian scriptures."*
*"And thus, it is the Atma or the spirit."*
*"It is without form, and people see it through its grace."*

Explanation: The spirit is referred to as the "least" because, compared to the physical body, it has the length of a human thumb, as described in the sacred Indian scriptures.

*"And so, it is the Atma or the spirit."*
*"It is without form, and people see it through its grace."*

Explanation: The spirit is without form and can be perceived by people through its grace.

*"The Purusha, who is ancient yet not old, is the soul of all, resides within everyone, and embraces everything. Those who know it do not enter into visible life on any world."*

Explanation: The Purusha, which refers to the divine spirit, is described as ancient and eternal. It is the essence or soul of all beings, residing within everyone and encompassing everything. Therefore, those who attain knowledge of the Purusha do not become entangled in any world's visible aspects of life.

*"Those who know God say about Him: He has no beginning, and He has no end, and He is from eternity.*
*"And two birds resemble a human being and oppose each other. But, nevertheless, both know each other and sit on the same tree. The difference between them is that one of them reaps the fruits of actions, indicated by the fruits of the trees, while the other does not grasp those fruits and is merely a spectator.*
*"The one who sits on that tree to receive the reward for his deeds and forgets his power is*

*bound by error and ignorance and becomes the target of sorrow.*

*"When he realizes his greatness and power, and when he knows that he is the individual soul (Dživatma) and nothing else, that he himself is the bird who is the Supreme Soul (Paramatma), then he is immediately freed from sorrow."*

Explanation: Those who have knowledge of God describe Him as eternal, without a beginning or end. The analogy of the two birds sitting on a tree is used to illustrate a distinction. One bird represents the individual soul, which experiences the consequences of its actions, while the other bird represents the Supreme Soul. The individual soul, when identified solely with its actions and forgetting its true power, becomes subject to sorrow. However, upon realizing its true nature and recognizing its unity with the Supreme Soul, it becomes liberated from sorrow.

*"He is the destroyer of everything. He is a great knower and knows all his creations. And he knows all the secrets of creatures. The whole world is in him, and he is the Lord of all two-legged and four-legged beings.*

*He is finer than the finest, he is in the innermost of the whole world, he renews the world, and all the various forms are his forms.*
*All the knowers and all the saints have united with him through realization, and because they also recognized him as the cause of their own bodies, they have torn apart the nets of death within themselves.*
*His name is supremely renowned.*
*What you see with your external eye is not his likeness, for you cannot see him with your external eyes. But when you reject everything that is apart from him, you can find him. You can find him through pure intellect or by recognizing yourself as his form. Those who have attained this vision are immortal."*

Explanation: Firstly, there is a mention of saints who have become immortal. It is necessary to explain to the child what saints and faithful sages, or adepts, are. An adept or great sage is one and the same. A true saint is only one whom God has made holy, that is, one with whom God has connected and thus made them sanctified and immortal.

All the great yogis in India are and have been saints in the true sense of the word. But there were and are saints in China, Tibet, Persia, and indeed throughout the entire East, and there were also saints in ancient Greece and Rome, although they were called sages there. Some such saints among the ancient European nations were, for example, Plato, Jamblichus, Pythagoras, and many others. In the Middle Ages, there were many Catholic and non-Catholic saints. Among the non-Catholic saints, for example, was the tremendous mystic Jakob Böhme. Many Catholic saints were not faithful saints because they were declared saints by people, namely the Pope and the College of Cardinals, who, as human beings, cannot and could not make anyone holy, even if they had the greatest external merits.

It is true that the assembly of cardinals, led by the Pope, carefully and extensively examines the life of a man or woman who is proposed to be declared a saint. It is true that they consider and study every action and, if applicable, the writings left behind, as almost every saint is declared a saint by the Church only after their death. In the Middle Ages and ancient times, martyrdom was a significant factor in the declaration of someone as a saint. However, all of this does not necessarily make a person a true saint.

A genuine and authentic saint must or must have been connected with God, permeated by divine power, and may have attained immortality even in their mortal body, and they must be an initiate while still alive. After death, one cannot attain sanctity or immortality if one has not achieved it while alive, while in the human body.

What the Church calls salvation is the attainment of immortality, but a saved person must already be alive and not only after death!

Among Catholic saints, there were indeed great adepts and initiates. Almost all the apostles who received sacred teachings directly from Jesus Christ can be mentioned, as well as many others, such as St. Francis of Assisi, St. Teresa, St. Bernard, St. John of the Cross, St. Dionysius, St. Augustine, who was also an outstanding philosopher, and countless others. However, someone like Emperor Charlemagne, who was declared a saint by the Church only because of his significant contributions to the spread of Christianity, was not a true saint.

The Catholic Church has hundreds of such false saints. But that doesn't matter because, on the contrary, Christianity has had and still has thousands of true saints, many of whom the Church doesn't even know about because they became saints without its knowledge and were never officially declared as saints.

Among them, there are many hermits who lived in seclusion and attained immortality without anyone knowing about it. I say "they are" because those who have attained immortality are still alive, even if they were born fifty thousand years ago or even longer. They exist within the divine and are connected with all the other saints of all times and all nations in an inseparable unity known as the "Brotherhood of the White Lodge."

In ancient times, saints were also high priests, such as in ancient Egypt, and the kings of ancient nations were saints. This is why the Egyptian civilization flourished for thousands of years because it was ruled by sages and initiates.

All these saints and initiates from around the world and throughout history have left us one excellent and straightforward teaching, one doctrine, and one commandment: to seek God within ourselves through the concentration of our thoughts and thereby become immortal.

Furthermore, we read above that His name is supremely glorious. This brings us to the second mystical practice, which is suitable for children from the age of seven onwards. Ramakrishna, one of the greatest saints of India, constantly emphasized the repetition of God's name and that through it, we attain salvation. This may seem contradictory to one of God's commandments, which states, "Do not take the name of God in vain!"

However, this commandment precisely means that we should not speak God's name aloud but rather repeat it constantly within our minds. This is the highest, purest, and most effective form of prayer.

However, God has countless names, so which name of God should we constantly think of within ourselves? In reality, a person could choose any name of God from any era. But the best and most appropriate is the name found in Jewish Kabbalah and the Bible, which is Jehovah. This word is actually composed of five vowels, and for the purpose of mystical practice, it is pronounced as I E O U A. Vowels are the foundation of human speech and words, and each of them possesses a unique mystical power that is awakened within a person as they begin to repeat this sacred name within themselves.

We must start with the feet because the feet must be penetrated first by the spirit of the letters in order to be "washed," as Christ said. This is sufficient for the child for now. Other reasons, which are described in the "Fire Bush," will be addressed later.

For the child, it is enough to focus their thoughts on both their feet and recite the letters I E O U A in their mind.

For a start, ten minutes a day is sufficient, just as children should practice concentration for only 10 minutes, even if they were practicing concentration on the little sun, as described earlier.

Now let us hear what the Upanishads say about the spirit residing in the human heart:

*"And that Dzivatma is the size of a thumb in the middle of the heart, and its light resembles the sun. Through reason, it has fallen into the bondage of the external self and external will."*

However, God has countless names, so which name of God should we constantly think within ourselves? In reality, a person could choose any name of God from any era. But the best and most appropriate is the name found in Jewish Kabbalah and the Bible, which is Jehovah. This word is actually composed of five vowels, and for the purpose of mystical practice, it is pronounced as I E O U A. Vowels are the foundation of human speech and words, and each of them possesses a unique mystical power that is awakened within a person as they begin to repeat this sacred name within themselves.

We must start with the feet because the feet must be penetrated first by the spirit of the letters in order to be "washed," as Christ said. This is sufficient for the child for now. Other reasons, which are described in the "Ohnivém Keři (Fire Bush), will be addressed later.

For the child, it is enough to focus their thoughts on both their feet and recite the letters I E O U A in their mind.

For a start, ten minutes a day is sufficient, just as children should practice concentration for only 10 minutes, even if they were practicing concentration on the little sun, as described earlier.

Now let us hear what the Upanishads say about the spirit residing in the human heart:

*"And that Dzivatma is the size of a thumb in the middle of the heart, and its light resembles the sun. Through reason, it has fallen into the bondage of the external self and external will."*
*"That light, which has the size of a thumb, is present in the hearts of most small creatures in the size of a needle's point, and in many creatures that are even smaller, it is like the tip of a hair when we divide it into a hundred times a hundred parts, and further divide that part into a hundred parts. It varies according to the size of the creatures, and that Dživatma corresponds to the size of their hearts."*

Explanation: This information could only be given by adepts who see the Spirit of God in all creatures. Thus, that divine spark exists in the smallest creatures with a size of one-millionth of a hair's thickness.

*"From the moment a person realizes themselves, they become immortal."*

*"And that Džívatma is not male, nor female, nor religious."*

*"After death, the Džívatma participates in joy as a reward corresponding to their actions when they assumed a body in the previous worlds. And in each state, they take on one dense body and one subtle body."*

Explanation: Every person has a dense physical body and a subtle astral body. But in a mystic, a new, subtle, immortal body is formed, which is of fiery essence and cannot be destroyed. This is expressed in the following sentence:

*"And the reward that follows good and bad actions and the reward that comes after contemplation is that the dense and subtle bodies unite."*

Explanation: When the dense and subtle bodies unite, it means incarnating in a particular world. Contemplation refers to mystical concentration, which gives rise to the immortal body. Those who have wholly attained the immortal body no longer need to incarnate into a physical body.

Finally, we present the instructions for the mystical path as stated in the Oupnek'hat:

*"The path to this is as follows: first, go to the teacher. Secondly, have faith in the teacher and in Brahma. Thirdly, listen to the truth from the teacher. Learn to prove the truth and immerse yourself constantly in true knowledge, which means being in continuous unity with the primordial. Finally, practice the eight methods of yoga and understand the consequences of every action in due time. Furthermore, be benevolent, patient, and pure, and always be joyful. Do not have personal will, and be generous. Embrace work with joy, avoid being plagued by envy, and surrender completely to Brahma. This will unite Dživatma with Atma, and you will be blessed."*

Explanation: The teacher refers to a guide whom we must trust just as we trust in God. If one cannot find a teacher, one can acquire books written by good teachers. Then it is necessary to hear the truth from the teacher and learn to prove that truth, not to others, but to oneself. Those who try to teach others from the beginning, even when they do not yet know the truth themselves, especially when they try to impose mystical teachings on others, make a great mistake. It is like a blind person trying to lead another blind person. Only when we are asked should we respond or show the way. Furthermore, it is urged to constantly immerse oneself in the primordial essence, which is the inner sun.

Regarding the eightfold path of yoga, it is not suitable for us as it is an Indian prescription associated with strict asceticism, which is impossible for us. Finally, there is the urging to expect the consequences of every action in due time. This is the fulfilling law of karma, but it can be forgiven for the mystic if it has not come into effect. Unfulfilled consequences can be forgiven according to the words of Christ, where we pray for the forgiveness of our sins.

In the end, the qualities that we should cultivate within ourselves are listed. The main one is to be joyful and to continue with our own will, carrying out our duties with a joyful mind. And in the end, attribute everything we do to God and never to people. Those who rely on people will always be disappointed. But God is an unshakable pillar that can never collapse. By relying on this pillar, we can achieve everything.

*"And this is the great mystery of Oupnek'hatu, which should be preserved. And those who preached this knowledge always came, but it should not be disclosed to those whose hearts have not reached peace. However, it should be told to a suitable son and a disciple with a pure heart."*

Explanation: This is the sacred teaching from the holy books of India that has endured for millennia and will last for eternity. Let us instill in our children respect for the holy books of all nations, not just the Bible. Let us teach them to understand the significance of this great mystery and impress upon them that few people know this teaching, and those who have understood it are the chosen ones of God and, according to the words of Christ, become true children of God!

# About the Author

Karel Weinfurter was born on May 27, 1867, in Jičín, Czech Republic, to his parents, Karel Weinfurter and Antonie Jiránková. His father, a soldier in the Austro-Hungarian army, left the family soon after Karel's birth. In 1880, the family moved to Prague, where his father worked as a merchant.

During his school years, Weinfurter became interested in spiritualism after learning about it from his religion teacher. Along with his friends, he attempted to communicate with spirits and develop mediumistic abilities based on various instructions. It is said that he even received prophecies from the "spirit realm" before the death of Crown Prince Rudolf. Weinfurter's fascination with spiritualism consumed him to the extent that he had to leave school and was briefly admitted to a psychiatric institution.

In 1890, Weinfurter joined a spiritualist circle where he met Baron Adolf Franz Leonhard and Gustav Meyrink, who later became well-known writer. Together with a few others, they founded the Theosophical Lodge "U modré hvězdy" (The Blue Star), dedicated to the study of Theosophy, Freemasonry, Rosicrucian literature, and Indian philosophy. They also gained access to the writings of various mystics, although their understanding of these works was limited at the time.

They were initiated into society by Friedrich Eckstein, a prominent figure in European Theosophy and occultism. Through Eckstein, they were introduced to the German teacher of

Christian mysticism, Mailänder, whom they accepted as their spiritual guide. Mailänder's teachings were mainly based on the works of Christian mystic Jakob Böhme and partially on Rosicrucian symbolism.

Weinfurter's early employment included working as a postal clerk and an assistant to an art dealer. He also served as a secretary to the poet Jaroslav Vrchlický. During this time, he began his career as a journalist, writing reviews and articles for various publications. He also worked as an office clerk and an assistant teacher at Charles-Ferdinand University in Prague.

Later, Weinfurter became a translator and editor for the publisher J.R. Vilímek. Translation became his primary source of income for most of his life. It was during this period that his first book, "Divy a kouzla indických fakirů" (Miracles and Magic of Indian Fakirs), was published in May 1913 by Vilímek. The book went through three editions.

In addition to his literary pursuits, Weinfurter had various interests and hobbies. He wrote articles on sports shooting, studied music and painting, and developed a fascination with entomology, the study of insects. His expertise in entomology led to the publication of a specialized work on microscopy, which was used as a reference in universities. He even discovered a new species of fly, which was named after him.

After World War I, Weinfurter began collaborating closely with the publisher Jan Zmatlík. He translated and published numerous works of occult and spiritual literature for Zmatlík's "Knihovna šťastných lidí" (Library of Happy People). In mid-1921, he started editing the magazine "Okultní a spiritualistická revue" (Occult and Spiritualist Review) for Zmatlík, which was the first Czech magazine to explore the synthesis of esotericism from different religious and philosophical systems. It was in this magazine that Weinfurter first published an article on mysticism, describing mystical exercises. The article received unexpected attention, leading to several follow-ups.

During this time, Weinfurter faced criticism from Otakar Gries, a hermeticist from Přerov, who claimed exclusive rights to the correct (magical) interpretation of so-called letter exercises. Weinfurter defended his mystical interpretation (which he had learned from his Rosicrucian teacher) in the magazine, but Gries continued his attacks. As a result, Weinfurter decided to step down from editing the magazine.

Upon Zmatlík's request, Weinfurter began working on a more extensive work on mysticism. Little did he know that his life was about to take a significant turn. On Easter of 1923, his book "Ohnivý keř čili odhalená cesta mystická" (The Fiery Bush or the Unveiled Mystic Path) was published. The book quickly sold out and sparked a newfound interest in mysticism. Some Catholic priests even acknowledged Weinfurter's work. Monks from various orders practiced the exercises outlined in his book, and there was a growing interest in mysticism within the church, leading to translations of works by previously overlooked saints into Czech. With the support of a patron, Weinfurter started publishing the magazine "Psyche," dedicated to mysticism, in 1924. A circle of enthusiasts formed around him, which eventually became the foundation of the emerging organization called "Psyché." The society emphasized practicing the mystical exercises from "Ohnivý keř" and prohibited other practices. In addition to lectures, the society published various publications, including Weinfurter's own writings and translations.

In 1937, British journalist and researcher Paul Brunton visited Prague at the invitation of the society. Weinfur ter translated and published several of Brunton's essential books. Through Brunton, Czech mystics learned about the teachings of Mahārshi, an Indian sage whose teachings became crucial for the further development of Czech mysticism. Weinfurter was the first to translate Mahārshi's essential works into Czech in 1940.

The period of mystical development was abruptly interrupted by the onset of World War II. During the Heydrich regime, Weinfurter was arrested and detained. Shortly after his release, he fell ill due to the cold conditions in his prison cell. He passed away on March 14, 1942, in Prague.

Weinfurter's literary legacy includes over 80 titles. While many of these were pamphlets or abridged versions of more significant works, his most well-known book remains "Ohnivý keř čili odhalená cesta mystická." The book went through multiple editions and had a significant impact on the interest in mysticism in the Czech Republic. He also wrote an eleven-volume series called "Bible ve světle mystiky" (Bible in the Light of Mysticism), which provided interpretations and commentaries on selected books of the New Testament and several apocryphal texts from a mystical perspective. His other notable works include "Mystický slabikář" (Mystical Primer), a two-volume interpretation of mystical dreams, symbols, and secret characters of the Rosicrucians, and "Mistr Rámakrišna" (Master Rāmakrishna), a comprehensive contribution to understanding the life and teachings of the prominent Indian saint.

Weinfurter's translations were equally significant for the field of mysticism. He translated over 300 books, including works by Rāmakrishna, Eckhart, de Molinos, Blavatsky, Brunton, and many others. His translations played a vital role in introducing Czech readers to a wide range of spiritual and mystical literature.

Weinfurter's mysticism was rooted in both Western and Eastern traditions. He drew inspiration from Western mystics such as

Eckhart, Suso, Tauler, Ruysbroeck, and Kempis, as well as heretical figures like Böhme and the Quietists. From the Eastern traditions, he incorporated the teachings of Rāmakrishna and his disciples, emphasizing the original Indian Vedānta. Weinfurter saw mysticism as a means of bridging the gap between Eastern and Western religions, advocating for their synthesis. His mysticism did not reject religion but rather stripped it of dogma and served as an overarching framework in which Eastern and Western mystics could find common ground.

Weinfurter's mystical teachings were seen as an alternative for those who were unsatisfied or disillusioned with traditional religious institutions. His works and translations influenced many individuals in the Czech Republic who were engaged in alternative, non-denominational mysticism, such as František Drtikol, Květoslav Minařík, Jiří Scheufler, and numerous others.

Karel Weinfurter's contributions to mysticism and his exploration of esoteric traditions left a lasting impact on the spiritual landscape of the Czech Republic. His writings continue to inspire and guide spiritual seekers, offering a synthesis of mystical wisdom from both the East and the West.

# Translator's Note

"Mysticism for All (Especially for Parents)" is a captivating translation of the Czech book "Mystika všem: (zvláště rodičům)" by Karel Weinfurter. Originally published in 1934, this edition has been skillfully translated by Kytka Hilmarova, allowing readers to delve into the profound teachings of Weinfurter.

In this enlightening work, Weinfurter explores the realms of mysticism, providing valuable insights and guidance for all individuals, with a particular emphasis on parents. Drawing from his extensive knowledge and expertise, Weinfurter unravels the mysteries of the spiritual world, shedding light on the hidden dimensions of existence.

This edition is a translation from the original publication by the Psyche Society in Prague in 1934. Through Kytka Hilmarova's translation, the essence of Weinfurter's teachings is brought to life, offering readers a deeper understanding of mysticism and its relevance to their lives.

"Mysticism for All (Especially for Parents)" serves as an invitation to embark on a transformative journey of self-discovery and spiritual growth. May this translation ignite curiosity and inspire readers to explore the profound wisdom of Karel Weinfurter's work.

# About the Translator

Kytka Hilmarová, a Prague native and political refugee, embarked on a transformative journey at a young age when she and her parents sought asylum in the United States in 1968. As an accomplished author, translator, and publisher, Hilmarová has left an indelible mark on the literary world, bridging the gap between Czech literature and English-speaking readers.

With over 200 books brought to life as a prolific ghostwriter and a portfolio of translating more than 100 Czech literary works into English, Hilmarová acts as a vital bridge connecting Czech literature with a global audience. Her visionary approach and unwavering commitment to preserving and promoting Czech culture, history, tradition, and literature have ensured that the legacy of Czech literary works remains alive, vibrant, and cherished for generations to come.

As the founder of Czech Revival Publishing, Hilmarová showcases the rich tapestry of Czech literary gems, fostering cultural exchange and expanding the global reach of Czech authors. Through her captivating works and translations, she invites readers to immerse themselves in the enchanting world of Czech literature, offering a glimpse into its diverse themes, profound emotions, and timeless wisdom.

Join Kytka Hilmarová on a literary journey that illuminates the treasures of Czech literature, history, and tradition. Her exceptional talent, resilience, and relentless pursuit of bridging cultures make her an indispensable figure in bringing the richness of

Czech literature to English-speaking audiences, ensuring its enduring legacy for years to come.

10% of book proceeds support the preservation of Czech culture in the United States. Learn more about our efforts to safeguard and enhance Czech traditions, language, arts, and history through the following:

Czechs in America Organization (CIAO) is dedicated to fostering the appreciation, understanding, and teaching of Czech culture and history. We exist to preserve, promote, and support efforts to perpetuate the Czech culture, history, customs, and traditions in the United States. CzechAmerica.org

The Czech Museum was established with the purpose of preserving, collecting, exhibiting, researching, and interpreting a collection of artifacts and archival material related to Czech history and culture. TheCzechMuseum.org

Everything Czech is dedicated to fostering a profound understanding and appreciation of the unique and vibrant history, culture, and traditions of the Czech people. EverythingCzech.com

www.ingramcontent.com/pod-product-compliance
Lightning Source LLC
LaVergne TN
LVHW011424080426
835512LV00005B/249